Welcome to an Amazing Year of Reading!

This book is like a library in your hand. It is filled with different texts and stories by award-winning authors and illustrators. Let's read on to find out more.

Reading and Writing Through *Wonders*

The more you read, the more you'll learn! You will spend time talking and writing about texts. You will explore how the books connect to you and your world.

Building Knowledge

Reading these texts will help you build knowledge about different topics. Each weekly text starts off with an **Essential Question**. This question helps you set a purpose for what you will learn from the text.

Essential Question

Your New Learning Partners

This book and your **Reading/Writing Companion** are connected. They work together as your partners in reading, writing, and thinking.

Reading/Writing Companion

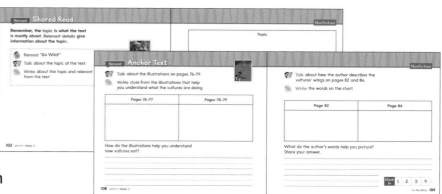

Literature Anthology

Once you learn new ideas, you will take that knowledge with you everywhere you go!

What You'll Read

You will find different types of texts, or genres, in this book. You will use what you learn about each genre in the Reading/Writing Companion to read these texts.

Realistic Fiction

Folktale

Fantasy

Opinion Text

Nonfiction

PLAY

Poetry

Personal Narrative

Biography

Wonders

Amazing Stories

You will read wonderful fiction stories. The stories include realistic fiction, fantasies, and folktales. Follow the characters through these exciting stories.

Powerful Poetry

You will read different poems. As you read poetry, listen to the rhyme and rhythm that help you understand the meaning of each poem.

Interesting Nonfiction

There are different kinds of nonfiction texts. They all teach us facts about a topic. You will see special features in texts, such as maps and photographs. These help you build more knowledge.

Sneak Peek at the Stories and Poems

This year, you will read great stories and poems.
They will help you see your world in new ways.

This year, you will read stories about friendship. In *Hi! Fly Guy* by **Tedd Arnold,** you'll read about how a pet can be a best friend. In *Lissy's Friends* by **Grace Lin,** you will read about a girl who makes new friends by sharing origami.

You will read stories about taking action. In *Rain School* by **James Rumford,** you'll read about children who build their own schoolhouse. In *Click, Clack, Moo: Cows That Type* by **Doreen Cronin,** you'll read about cows who want a better life on their farm.

You will read poems about family and friends. In *Abuelita's Lap* by **Pat Mora,** you'll read about a boy who spends time with his grandmother. In *There Are Days and There Are Days* by **Beatrice Schenk de Regniers,** you'll read about the fun you can have being with friends and by yourself, too.

You will read stories about exploring the world around you. In *Kitten's First Full Moon* by **Kevin Henkes,** you'll read about a curious kitten who wants to get to the Moon.

Sneak Peek at the Nonfiction Texts

Wonders is filled with texts that will help you build knowledge about science and social studies.

You will read texts about animals and how they survive in nature. In ***Vulture View,*** **April Pulley Sayre** tells how vultures use their bodies to find food.

You will read texts about history. In ***Long Ago and Now*** by **Minda Novek,** you'll learn about how things in the past were similar to or different from our lives today.

Bettmann/Getty Images

You will read about exploring the world. In *The Moon,* you'll read about how a telescope helps us see the Moon up close. In *Building Bridges,* you'll learn how engineers build different kinds of bridges.

You will learn about important issues. You will read about taking care of bees in **"Save Our Bees!"** and volunteering in **"Be a Volunteer!"** You will read the authors' opinions about the topics. This will help you form your own opinions.

The best way to learn about things that interest you is to do a lot of reading.

"Let's get reading!"

THE BIG CONCEPT

Getting to Know Us

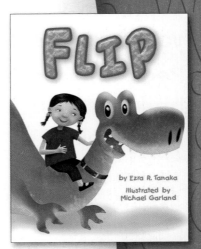

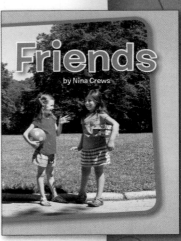

(c) Nina Crews (b) SerrNovik/iStock/Getty Images

Genre Realistic Fiction

Essential Question

What do you do at your school?

Read about a boy who brings a special friend to school.

Go Digital!

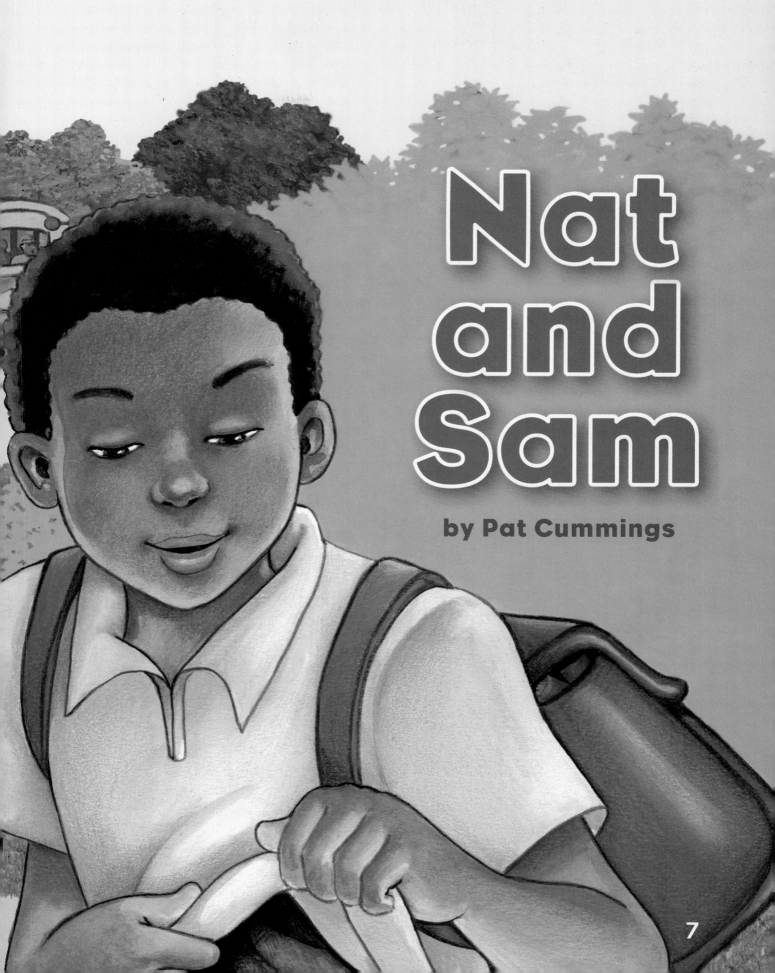

Nat and Sam

by Pat Cummings

Nat is at **school**.

Nat sat.

What does Nat have?

cat
can
pan
tan
tap

Nat has Sam.

Nat does **not** have Sam!

Sam sat.

Sam is with Pam.

Look! Sam can read.

Can Nat? Nat can.

Nat and Sam like school.

Meet Pat Cummings

Pat Cummings moved a lot when she was growing up, so she understands why Nat would bring an old friend to a new place. She loves to draw and write stories. And like Nat and Sam, she loves to read a good book.

Author's Purpose

Pat Cummings wanted to tell a story about a boy and the things he does at school. Draw a picture of something you do at school.

18

Respond to the Text

Retell

Use your own words to retell *Nat and Sam.* Information from your Character chart may help you.

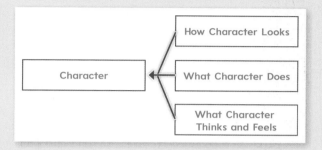

		How Character Looks
Character	←	What Character Does
		What Character Thinks and Feels

Write

Why did Nat's feelings about school change? Use these sentence frames:

> I read that Nat feels...
> I know that changes because...

Make Connections

COLLABORATE

What does Nat do that you can do at school, too?

ESSENTIAL QUESTION

Compare Texts
Read about how kids follow the rules at their school.

Rules at School

Our School Rules

Why do we have **rules** at school?

Rules can help us get along.
Rules can help us stay safe.

We raise our hands.

Shuart Pearce/Pixtal/age fotostock

We listen quietly.

We **obey** **safety** rules.

We let everyone play!
What are your school rules?

 Make Connections

Why is it important to have rules at school? **Essential Question**

Essential Question

What is it like where you live?

Read about a squirrel's day out in the city.

Go Digital!

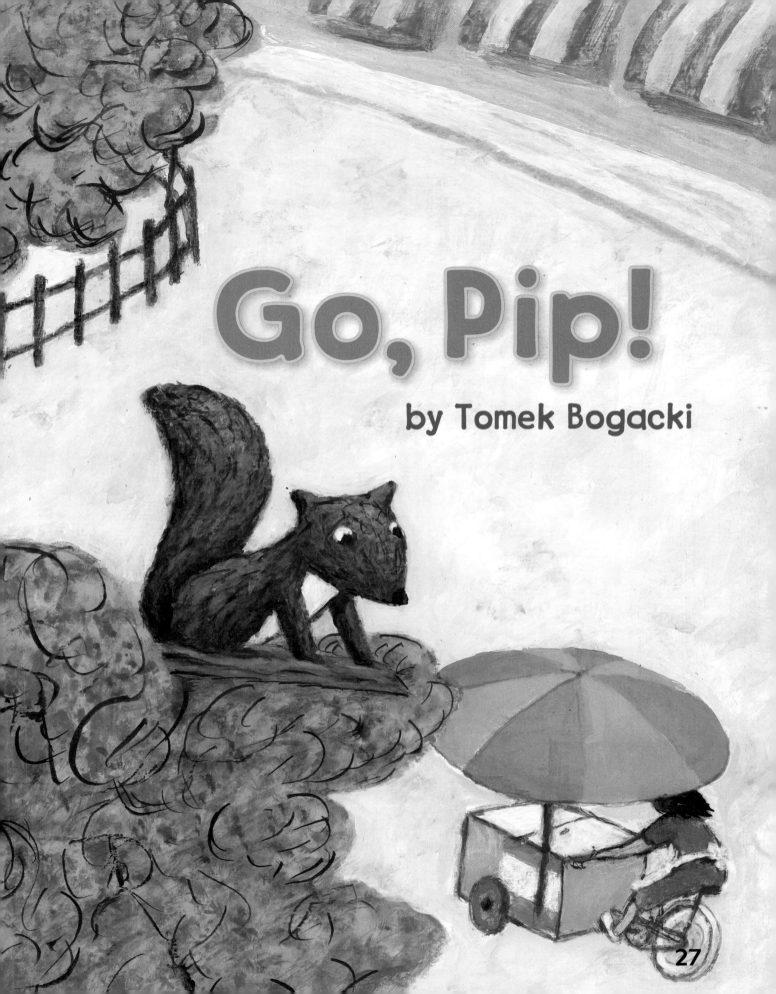

Go, Pip!

by Tomek Bogacki

Pip sits. Pip looks.

Pip can jump!

Pip is **out**.

Go, Pip!

Pip looks **up**.
It is **very** big.

Pip can look **down**.

Pip will go in.

Will this hat fit Pip?
It will!

Pip will go here.

Pip can look.

Where will Pip go?

Pip will go home!

Meet Tomek Bogacki

Tomek Bogacki used to live in a house in the forest. He liked to watch the animals there and draw pictures of them. Now he lives in a city where he likes to walk along the streets, visit museums, and watch squirrels in the park.

Tomek Bogacki

Author's Purpose

Tomek Bogacki wanted to tell a story about a curious squirrel who visits a city. Draw an animal visiting where you live. What might it see there?

Respond to the Text

Retell

Use your own words to retell *Go, Pip!* Information from your Character chart may help you.

Character	→	How Character Looks
		What Character Does
		What Character Thinks and Feels

Write

How does Pip feel about his neighborhood? Use these sentence starters:

> I read that Pip...
> The words and illustrations help me know that Pip...

Make Connections

 What other fun things could Pip do in a city?

ESSENTIAL QUESTION

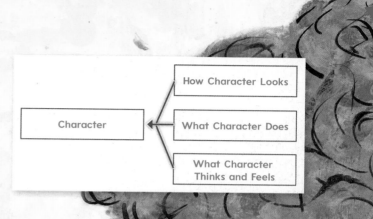

Compare Texts

Read about what it's like to live in the city.

A Surprise in the City

Hi! My name is Zoë.
I live in the **city**.
This is my **building**.

I look out my window.
I am excited!
Mom has a surprise for me today.

We go to the **playground**.
I play on the swings.
Is **this** my surprise?
Mom says no.

I learn a new jump at gymnastics.
Is **this** my surprise?
Mom says no.

Mom buys me a pretzel.
Is **this** my surprise?
Mom says no.

We stop at the pencil store.
This is my surprise!
I buy lots of pencils.
I **love** my surprise!

Make Connections

What is similar about the places Zoë and Pip visit?

Essential Question

Essential Question

What makes a pet special?

Read about a very unusual pet who goes to school.

Go Digital!

48

FLIP

by Ezra R. Tanaka

illustrated by
Michael Garland

Flip is my pet.
Flip is big.

Flip can not go in.
Flip is sad.

Flip **pulls** me in.

Flip and I go to class.

Flip sits.
Be good, Flip!

54

Flip likes class.

The kids like Flip.

Miss Black is mad.
Sit down, Flip!

Look at Miss Black!

Flip has a plan.

Flip did it!
The class claps.

Can Flip **come** back?
"Flip can," said Miss Black.
Flip is glad!

Meet the Illustrator

When Michael Garland was a child, he loved drawing characters from movies and books. Some of his favorite movies and books had funny creatures in them. So he drew a lot of dinosaurs just like Flip!

Illustrator's Purpose

Michael Garland likes to draw dinosaurs. Draw a dinosaur. Label your drawing.

Michael Garland

62

Respond to the Text

Retell

Use your own words to retell *Flip*. Tell who the characters are, where they are, and what happens to them.

Character	Setting	Events

Write

Think about Flip. Write what might happen the next day when Flip goes to school. Use these sentence frames:

The next day, Flip...
At school, he...

Make Connections

COLLABORATE

How is Flip special?
ESSENTIAL QUESTION

iguana

What Pets Need

What do pets **need**?

parrot

hamster

Like all **living things**, pets need food.
Some pets eat seeds or plants.

kittens

Some pets eat meat or fish.
All pets need fresh water.

dog

Pets need a safe home.
Pets need our love and **care**.

Make Connections

What do you think Flip
needs? **Essential Question**

Essential Question

What do friends do together?

Read about how two friends have fun together.

Go Digital!

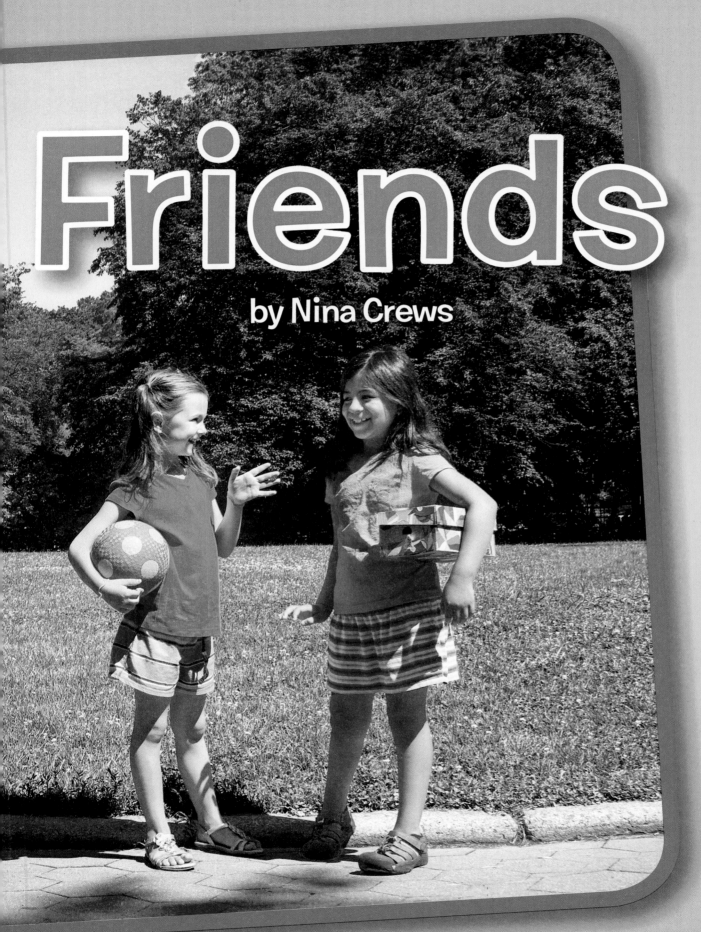

Friends

by Nina Crews

Pam and Jill are friends.
They play a lot.

Pam and Jill toss a ball.

Pam hops.
Jill hops, **too**!

They play tag.
Pam is quick.

73

Jill is not as quick as Pam.

Jill is hot.
She does not like tag.

Pam **makes** a plan.
She has a box.

Jill looks in.
It is a doll and a dog!

Pam and Jill sit on a rock.
They make up a game.

The dog and doll are friends.

Pam and Jill play, play, play.

It is a **fun** day!

Meet Nina Crews

Nina Crews uses photographs to tell stories about children. The children in the photographs are her family or friends. She says that her readers like to see pictures of real children.

Nina Crews

Author's Purpose

Nina Crews wanted to tell about real things friends do when they play together. Draw a picture of you and a friend playing.

Respond to the Text

Retell

Use your own words to retell the topic and relevant details in *Friends*.

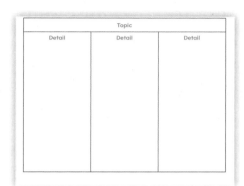

Write

Why is Pam a good friend to Jill? Use these sentence frames:

> Pam is a good friend because...
> She helps Jill by...

Make Connections
COLLABORATE

What can friends do when they want to play different games?

ESSENTIAL QUESTION

There Are Days And There Are Days

by Beatrice Schenk de Regniers

There are days I want to be
all alone
with only me
for company—
me and my cat.
There <u>are</u> days like that.

And there are days
(many more)
I don't want to be alone
any more.
Then
it seems to me
jokes are funnier,
honey's honey-er,
sun is sunnier
when
I'm with a friend!

Make Connections

What does the boy like about being with a friend? **Essential Question**

Essential Question

How does your body move?

Read about the fun ways kids can move.

Go Digital!

Move It!

How can kids **move**?
We can move in lots of ways.
We use our bodies to help us.

I can **run**.
I have strong legs.
They help me go fast.

legs

Masterfile

feet

I can **jump**.
I pick up my feet.
I will land on the grass.

I can catch.
I use **two** hands.
I can grab the ball.

hands

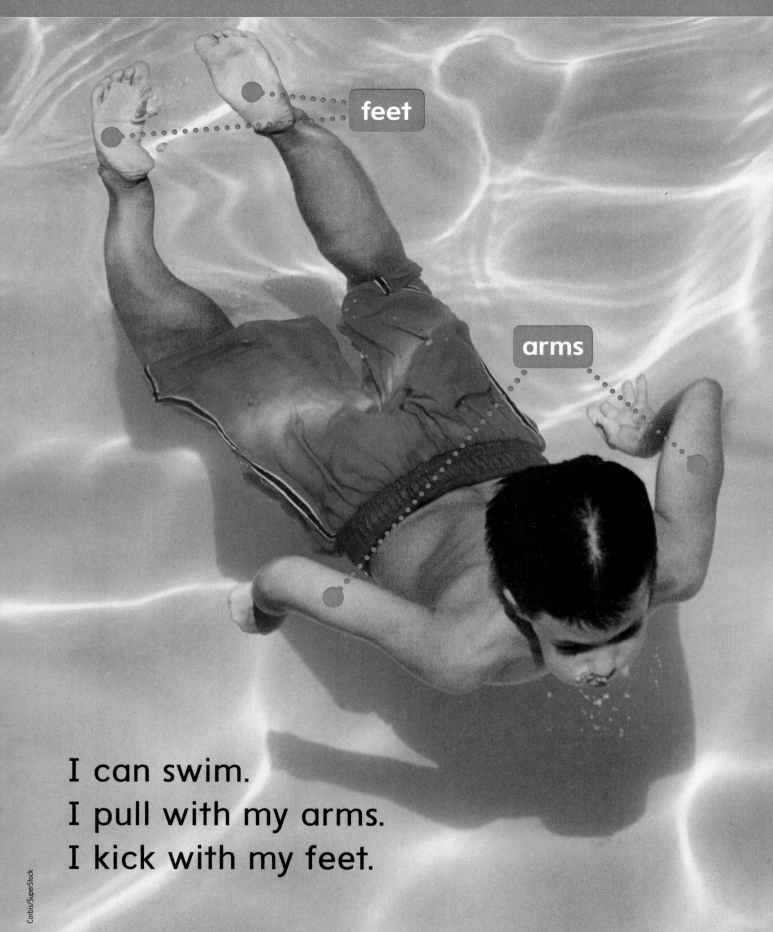

feet

arms

I can swim.
I pull with my arms.
I kick with my feet.

I can spin this hoop.
I move my hips fast.
This helps it stay up.

hips

I can do fun tricks.
There are lots of ways to move!
What can you do?

Respond to the Text

1. Use relevant details from the selection to retell the text. RETELL

2. What's your favorite thing to do outside? Add a new page to the text. WRITE

3. What else do your arms help you to do? TEXT TO WORLD

Compare Texts
Read about how one family likes to move.

My Family Hike

Hi! My name is Otto.
Today I'm going **hiking**.
I will look for snakes on the trail.
I grab my hat and water bottle.

We drive to the trail.

My sister and I want to be first.

I **start** to look for snakes.

I search for anything moving.

Soon I'm hot and out of **breath**.
I **climb** on a rock to get a better view.
I see a snake!
It slips away and hides near a tree.

Finally we stop.
There are tall trees all around us.
We made it to the top of the mountain!
I will look for **another** snake!

Make Connections

How does this family like to move?

Essential Question

Glossary

What is a Glossary? A glossary can help you find the meanings of words. The words are listed in alphabetical order. You can look up a word and read it in a sentence. Sometimes there is a picture to help you.

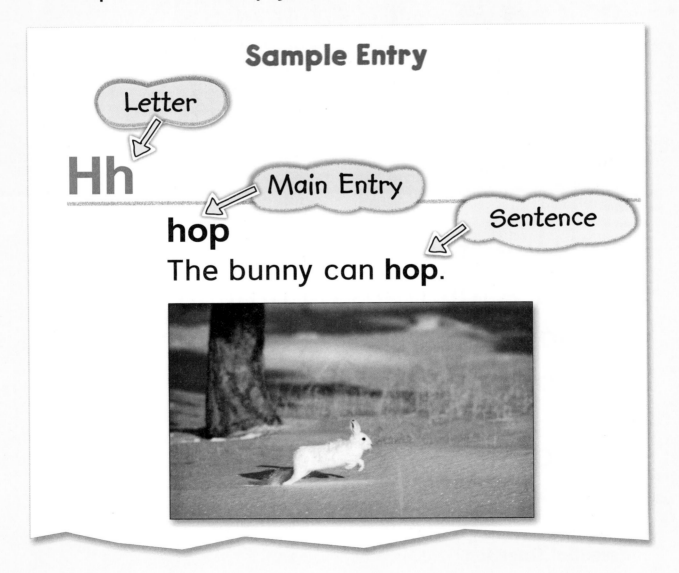

Sample Entry

Letter

Hh

Main Entry

Sentence

hop

The bunny can **hop**.

Bb

big
A hippo is **big**.

Cc

clap
Kim and Roz **clap**.

Dd

doll

I hug my **doll**.

Gg

good

This is **good** for me.

Hh

hat

This **hat** is red.

hop

The bunny can **hop**.

Mm

move

We **move** around and around.

Pp

pull

We **pull** on the rope.

Rr

run
It is fun to **run** in a race.

Ss

school
Our **school** is very big.

(t)Martin Barraud/OJO Images/Getty Images; (b) Thomas Barwick/Digital Vision/Getty Images

sit

The kids **sit** in a circle.

Tt

trick

We can see the **trick**.